THE EXERCISE OF ARMES

THE EXERCISE OF ARMES

A SEVENTEENTH CENTURY
MILITARY MANUAL

Jacob de Gheyn

New, English Language Edition
EDITED BY DAVID J. BLACKMORE,
ROYAL ARMOURIES
HM TOWER OF LONDON

Greenhill Books

**Greenhill
Books**

This edition of *The Exercise of Armes*
first published 1986 by Greenhill Books,
Lionel Leventhal Limited, 2-6 Hampstead High Street,
London NW3 1QQ

This edition © Lionel Leventhal Limited, 1986

ISBN 0-947898-45-X

Publishing History
The Exercise of Armes by Jacob de Gheyn
was first published in 1607 as *Wapenhandelinghe
van Roers Musquetten Ende Spiessen*

Printed by Paradigm Print,
Gateshead, Tyne and Wear

CONTENTS

INTRODUCTION

This is a book for all with an interest in the English Civil War, the Thirty Years War and Medieval Warfare.

The first edition of Jacob de Gheyn's drill book, *Wapenhandelinghe van Roers Musquetten ende Spiessen*, first appeared in 1607, although the illustrations were produced some time before that, perhaps as early as 1595. However, the book proved to be very popular and many editions were printed and the illustrations pirated many times, resulting in the drill shown by de Gheyn becoming common throughout Europe.

Just as the early editions and those that copied it were intended for the education of the soldier in the handling of his arms so it is with this edition. In this condensed handier size it is hoped that de Gheyn's influence upon drill will be seen again, this time amongst the ranks of the many people involved in re-enacting the English Civil Wars, for although it dates from at least thirty-five years before the outbreak of the civil wars the drill it illustrates was still relevant.

By the 1640s the caliver had become obsolete, but de Gheyn's drill for it demonstrates clearly how to load and fire any matchlock gun using powder flasks, whether carried on a porte-tache as illustrated or merely slung over the shoulder on cords. Similarly the drill for the musket, using a bandoleer, is the same with or without the musket rest which went out of use during the 1640s.

Pike drill of course remained constant throughout the seventeenth century and the illustrations of pike drill should help to make clear some of the more complex movements or postures.

This new edition, however, will also be of use to the military historian for whom a knowledge of the drill used can make the understanding of warfare so much easier; not just of the English Civil Wars but also of the Thirty Years War that ravaged Europe during the first half of the seventeenth century.

Finally, I am sure that anyone simply interested in arms, armour and costume will find each one of these illustrations an absolute delight.

David Blackmore,
Royal Armouries, HM Tower of London.
1986

Section 1

CALIVER DRILL

Shoulder your piece

Unshoulder your piece (the first motion)

And with the right hand hold it up (the second motion)

15

In the left hand take your piece

17

Take your match in your right hand

Blow your match

Cock your match

Try your match (to ensure that it will fall into
the priming pan)

25

Blow your match (covering the closed pan
with the two fore-fingers against sparks) and
then open your pan

Present your piece (the first motion, bringing
the muzzle down, not up)

The piece being presented, give fire

Take down your piece and balance it in your
left hand, the muzzle up in the air

Uncock your match

Return the match to your left hand

Blow out the pan and take hold of your
priming flask

Prime your pan

Close your pan

Shake off any loose powder

Blow off any loose powder

Cast about your piece to your left side (the first motion)

49

Balance the piece on your left side and take
hold of your powder flask

51

Open your charge

Charge your piece

Draw out your scouring-stick

Shorten your grip on your scouring stick (to hold it near your body) and load with a ball (taken with the right hand from your mouth or bullet bag)   59

Return your charge

Withdraw your scouring stick

Shorten your scouring stick

Replace your scouring stick

Shoulder your piece (the first motion)

Shoulder your piece (the second motion)

Shoulder your piece (the third motion)

The piece shouldered (as in figure 1)

75

Unshoulder your piece

And in the left hand let it sink

Hold your piece well

With the left hand alone hold your piece

Take your match in your right hand

Blow your match

Cock your match

Try your match

Guard your pan and stand ready

Section 2

MUSKET DRILL

March with the musket shouldered, the rest in your hand

97

March, and with the musket carry the rest

Unshoulder your musket

101

Hold your musket in the right hand and let it
sink into the left

103

In your left hand hold your musket and carry
your rest with it

Take your match in the right hand

Blow your match

Cock your match

Try your match

Guard your pan and blow your match

Hold up your musket and present

Give fire

119

Take down your musket and carry it with your   rest

121

Uncock your match

Place your match in your left hand

Blow out your pan

Prime your pan

Shut your pan

131

Cast off your loose powder

133

Blow off your loose powder

Cast about your musket

137

Trail your rest

Open your charge

Charge your musket

Draw out your scouring stick

Shorten your scouring stick and load your ball

Ram home your charge

Withdraw your scouring stick

Shorten your scouring stick

Replace your scouring stick

155

Bring your musket forward with the left hand

Hold your musket in your right hand and
recover your rest

159

Shoulder your musket

March and carry your rest with your musket

163

Unshoulder your musket

165

Lay your musket in the rest

Hold your musket on the rest

Balance your musket in the rest with your left
hand, leaving the right hand free

171

Take your match in the right hand

Blow your match

175

Cock your match

Try your match

179

Guard your pan and be ready

181

Section 3

PIKE DRILL

The pike ordered

Advance your pike (the first motion)

Advance your pike (the second motion)

The pike advanced

Order your pike (the first motion)

Order your pike (the second motion)

195

The pike ordered

Shoulder your pike (the first motion)

199

Shoulder your pike (the second motion)

The pike shouldered and carried level

The pike shouldered and carried sloping

Port your pike (the first motion)

Port your pike (the second motion)

Charge your pike

Order your pike (the first motion)

Order your pike (the second motion)

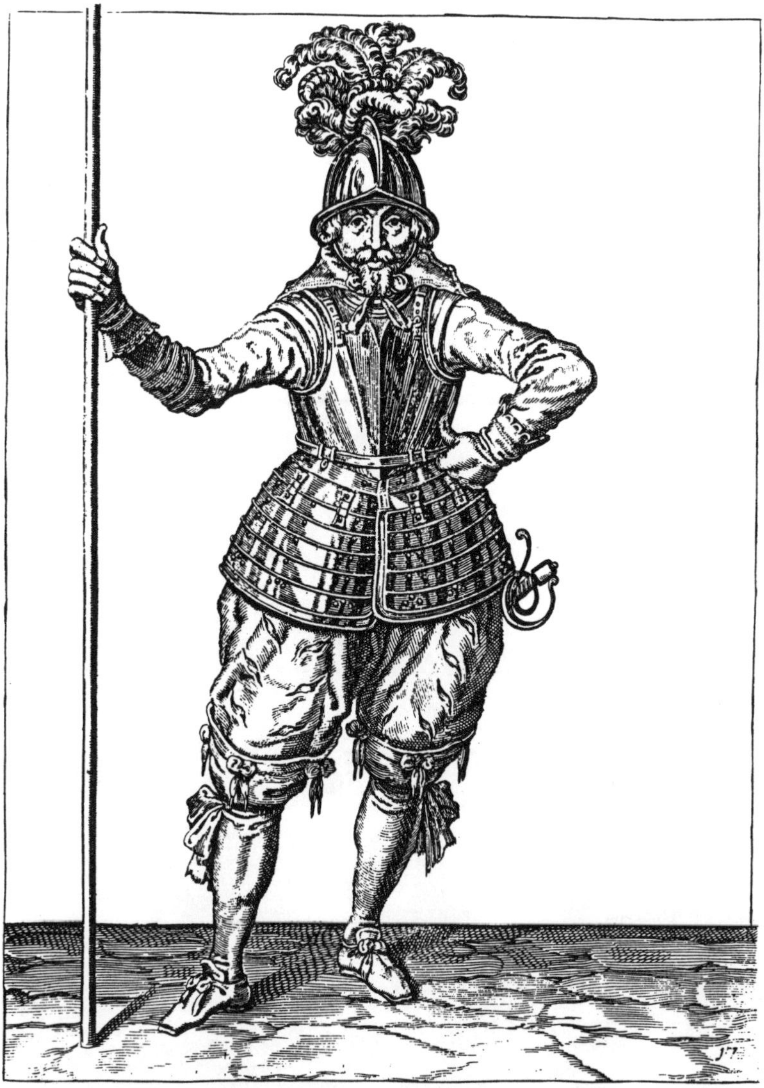

The pike ordered

The pike advanced

The pike charged (in one motion
from the advance)

221

Cheek your pike

Trail your pike

Charge your pike by palming it forward

Continue palming the pike forward

The pike charged

Charge your pike for horse and draw your sword

26

The pike being shouldered, charge your pike to the rear

The first motion

237

The second motion

The third motion, the pike charged

Face about and shoulder your pike (the first motion)

The second motion

The third motion, the pike shouldered

247